INTERVIEW / ENTREVISTA

Gil Kofman

I0139967

BROADWAY PLAY PUBLISHING INC
New York
www.broadwayplaypublishing.com
info@broadwayplaypublishing.com

INTERVIEW/ENTREVISTA
© Copyright 2011 by Gil Kofman

First printing: July 2011
I S B N: 978-0-88145-470-3

Book design: Marie Donovan
Typographic controls & page make-up: Adobe InDesign
Typeface: Palatino
Printed and bound in the U S A

ABOUT THE AUTHOR

Gil Kofman was born in Nigeria and raised in Kenya, Israel, and N Y C. He studied physics at Cornell before attending N Y U Graduate Film School, and later getting an M F A in playwriting from the Yale School of Drama.

Kofman's play AMERICAN MAGIC, a dark political satire, was produced in N Y, L A, and London with music by Lee Ranaldo from Sonic Youth and Richard Foreman playing the part of the President. It was published by Broadway Play Publishing Inc. Other plays, THE REPORT and PHARMACOPEIA were produced at the Evidence Room in L A. PHARMACOPEIA is also published by Broadway Play Publishing Inc. INTERVIEW/ENTREVISTA won a Dramalogue Award in L A and was later produced at the Dallas Theater Center. Previous plays were produced at C B G B, Workhouse Theater, Adobe Theater Company in N Y C, plus theaters in Chicago and Canada.

Gil has also published short fiction in Gordon Lish's *The Quarterly* and helped produce, edit and shoot the Sundance award Winning documentary, *Derrida*.

Gil also wrote and directed the feature film *The Memory Thief* which *The New York Times* called "morally audacious and intriguingly original." www. memorythiefmovie.com

He recently co-edited Ry Russo-Young's film *You Won't Miss Me* (Sundance 2009) which won a Gotham Award and played at various festivals throughout the world including SXSW, BAM, etc. And, he helped shoot verite camera for Kirby Dick's *Outrage* (Tribeca 2009 and aired on H B O with Magnolia distributing. Emmy nomination.)

His photos have sold through the Bonomo Gallery in Rome. And he's just finishing his first novel, called *acKursed!*. His most recent effort is directing a feature thriller in China called *Case Sensitive,* due for release in June.

INTERVIEW/ENTREVISTA was orginally produced
by Padua Playwrights in L A in 1995. The cast and
creative contributors were:

MAN...Frank Wood
WOMAN..Kadina de Elejalde
LARS... Jeff Phillips

Direction & design.. Gil Kofman

The play was then produced by Dallas Theater Center
in 1996. The cast and creative contributors were:

MAN...Frank Wood
WOMAN..Dolores Ferraro
LARS...Joe Goodrich

Direction .... Jonathon Mascone
Design ....John Binkley

CHARACTERS & SETTING

LARS
MAN
WOMAN

A nondescript room

dedicated to my three favorite sisters

(Scene: A nondescript room. A desk. Door. Window)

(MAN stands by window. Refilling the birdfeeder. Sound of plane passing overhead)

(LARS guards the door, a notepad in his hand.)

(WOMAN sits anxiously at desk, crossing and uncrossing her legs. Waiting. Another plane passes outside.)

(MAN at window, casually to WOMAN)

MAN: You say your husband is here.

WOMAN: Brother.

MAN: Excuse me...?

WOMAN: My brother.

MAN: Ah...yes. Sorry.

WOMAN: That's what I was told.

MAN: Who told you?

(Silence)

(MAN turns from window to face WOMAN, less kind.)

MAN: Who told you?

WOMAN: I...don't remember.

MAN: *(Crosses to desk)* You can trust us. Don't you trust us? *(Beat)* Lars...I don't think this woman trusts us.

(LARS shakes his head gravely.)

MAN: Why don't you trust us?

WOMAN: Look, I don't remember.

MAN: Was it your neighbor who told you?

WOMAN: I don't think so...no.

MAN: Well maybe we can help you remember. Would you like that? Would you like us to help you?

(Silence)

WOMAN: Please. I...

MAN: Your English is quite good. Isn't it Lars?

LARS: *(Perverse relish) Muy bien.*

MAN: Makes my job so much easier. Tell me something...

WOMAN: *(Overlapping)* I just want to see my brother...

MAN: *(Picks up binoculars)* You like birds? Watching them fly? Seeing their intelligence at work. Fascinating creatures. Always on the move, very very alert. If it were up to me I'd like to come back as one, preferably a hawk or some graceful sort of peregrine—any bird would do really, long as its not a vulture. Rather vulgar, aren't they? Vultures. Not very well liked. In the old days, you know, Greek prophets used to divine the future by studying the entrails of various animals and observing the careful flight of birds—which way they went, how they divided the sky with their wings. Today of course we have all sorts of airplanes... birds, airplanes... it's all confused up there and sometimes these birds get in the way of these planes...right inside the engines, allowing for major disasters... Anyway, I love them. Birds. *(He offers her binoculars.)* Care to have a look?

WOMAN: *(She demurs.)* Really, I came after my brother... see how he is...

MAN: *(Overlap)* Could it be that you find birds frightening? Their migratory habits unsettling? Some people do you know. Quite a few actually. They say it's inexplicable, their fear. Are you one of those frightened people?

(WOMAN looks down.)

MAN: Lars, this woman appear frightened to you?

LARS: She looks uncomfortable, sir.

MAN: Did you hear that?

(A plane passes overhead.)

MAN: I asked did you hear that?

WOMAN: Yes.

MAN: *(Normal voice)* Why are you so uncomfortable?

WOMAN: I...don't...know...

MAN: Have you done something wrong? Are you hiding something from us? What have you done?

WOMAN: It's about my brother.

MAN: Someone told you he was here.

WOMAN: Yes...I just...

MAN: *(Cutting her off)* Otherwise you wouldn't be here. We wouldn't have this fortunate chance to meet. Get better acquainted. Aren't you glad we had this opportunity? You and I...and Lars. Have you met Lars yet? Have you two been...introduced?

WOMAN: No...I...no...

(LARS crosses to shake WOMAN's hand.)

LARS: *(Lewdly)* Encantado conocerla.

(But LARS doesn't let go. Instead he continues to admire WOMAN's hand in his.)

MAN: Oh I've got it!! Maybe the sister told you. Yes, he has a sister you know. Perhaps she's the one who told you he was here?

WOMAN: But I am his sister.

(WOMAN *tries to work her hand free from* LARS. *No go*)

MAN: Oh...? I thought you were his wife.

WOMAN: No. I'm his sister. I told you that.

MAN: Did you?

WOMAN: I even showed you my...papers.

MAN: Papers...?

WOMAN: Documents.

MAN: Show me again.

(LARS *lets go of* WOMAN's *hand. She takes out some papers. Hands them to him, who hands them to* MAN, *who without inspecting them, hands them back to* LARS.)

MAN: All in order I take it?

WOMAN: Yes...last I looked I...

MAN: *(Ignoring her)* Lars...

LARS: Hard to tell sir. Could be forged, you know.

WOMAN: Oh no, I assure you....

(MAN *snaps fingers authoritatively.*)

MAN: Lars!!

(LARS *responds by viciously tearing up the papers.*)

WOMAN: You...you can't do that.

MAN: Like fuck I can't. *(Very deliberate)* Who the fuck are you?!

WOMAN: I told you.

MAN: His sister....

WOMAN: Yes.

(LARS *chuckles.*)

MAN: You are very stubborn. Are all your people this stubborn?

WOMAN: It's the truth.

MAN: That's no reason to be so unyielding.
Is it? Is it…?!

(MAN *studies* WOMAN. *Considering*)

MAN: When I look at you, sitting in that chair, it gives
me pause, it really does, it gives me pause and that
makes me think. (*He stares at her.*) Want to know what I
think about when I see you there? Sitting in that chair,
legs casually crossed, arms dropped awkwardly in
your lap? Don thinks…

LARS: That's him.

MAN: I'm Don—

LARS: He thinks…

MAN: What was she—

LARS: Meaning you…

MAN: What was she like as a little girl…that's what
I contemplate and think about. What was she really
like? This grown up woman sitting here in my office.
My chair. Profiled by the incredibly unflattering
incandescence of my desk lamp… What was she like
when she was growing up, this woman?

(LARS *produces a digital camera and snaps several photos of
the* WOMAN. *She's not sure how to react.*)

MAN: Not what you looked like, mind you, I couldn't
give a shit about that. But what were you like? As a
child. Happy? Sad? Painfully shy and withdrawn? An
odd combination of all three…? And where is she now,
this blithely innocent girl from our past? Is she still
here? In our midst? Are you in fact her…?

(LARS *flashes a few more pics.*)

MAN: Do you, by any chance, miss her? This little girl.
And if so, why are you concealing her from us? Are
you embarrassed? Afraid? Does she still visit you, this
girl from your past? Does she make the occasional

nocturnal visit when you least expect it and are just about to write her off in a pique of anger? And what do you talk about when she does appear? What activities do you two engage in? Do you tell her things you can't tell me as you sit here now bathed in the filthy impoverished light from my desk.

(LARS *reconfigures the light, snaps a few more photos.*)

WOMAN: I'm not sure I understand...

MAN: No?

WOMAN: I came here because I thought you might help me. I thought you...

MAN: Of course. Why else would you come.

WOMAN: *(Inserting)* Will you?

MAN: *(Overlap)* Of course.

WOMAN: Help me?

MAN: For me, to help you, I'll need full disclosure. You understand that.

LARS: *(Barking a la paparazzi)* Over here!! Right here!!

(*Briefly stealing* WOMAN's *attention,* LARS *snaps another picture.*)

MAN: That is...assuming I can help.

WOMAN: Thank you. You don't know what that would mean to me. What I've been through to get here.

MAN: But it's not always that easy. The people who come here...very hard to verify between who they are and who they say they are. You'd be surprised how a person changes when they drastically need something. And, well, a man in my position, my tenure, a man like me has to know precisely who he's dealing with at all times.

WOMAN: I would never try to deceive you...

MAN: No. Not intentionally.

WOMAN: It would work against my better interest.

MAN: Your so-called…provenance…must be infallible, beyond reproach.

WOMAN: I understand.

MAN: No shadows hiding in the shade.

WOMAN: No.

MAN: You must be entirely transparent.

LARS: *(With relish)* Naaaked.

MAN: Like a clean plate of glass that attracts the unfortunate bird to its premature death.

LARS: *(Clapping hands)* SPLAT!

MAN: Identity seems so obvious from the outside looking in. So self-evident it's almost deceptive. *(Beat)* I am a man. Ipso facto you are a woman. And Lars… Lars is my…bitch.

LARS: Thank you, sir.

MAN: But there is much more here than meets the reflexive eye. And for every thousand pictures we take, there is only one…

LARS: Sometimes two.

MAN: …that catches a glimmer of truth.

LARS: *(Snapping, proudly)* That's why we went digital.

MAN: And even then there is so much that is absent from the photo. From the shiny surface that is just another glossy lie.

(LARS takes a photo of himself next to the WOMAN. His smile even more grotesque by contrast to her discomfort.)

MAN: For example, here's a mental picture I often think about. A picture that haunts me almost every day of my life. Just as I'm about to drift into sleep…

(He removes a half-eaten sandwich and takes a bite.) As I
close my eyes, I'll often recall the public park where
I take my lunch during the day... and where this one
particular girl is always sitting alone on the swings.
The image is invariably tinged with melancholy and
I think to myself I think— All grown up, as a mature
handsome woman, what will this young little girl do
with her life? Where will she go, who will she marry?
Will she ever find herself here in my office, one day,
like you, illuminated by the unhealthy autumnal glow
of my desk lamp?

WOMAN: Please...I think you are confusing me with
someone else here.

MAN: I doubt that, seeing as how I'm now speaking in
a strictly hypothetical mode, I highly doubt that.

WOMAN: But this girl, is she real?

MAN: Oh yes. Quite real. In fact, she was there today.
Gave her the other half of my sandwich and thought
of you... or someone like you... now that I've met you.
*(He finishes sandwich, throws away wrapper. Then takes the
camera and reviews the photos* LARS *just took. Looking from
photo to* WOMAN *and back again.)*

MAN: Everything's a puzzle when you interpret the
world like I do. *(To* LARS, *re photo)* Delete.

LARS: I still need to edit them.

MAN: Will she have many friends? I ask myself. Or
turn senselessly schizophrenic with dark suicidal
ideations. Only time will tell. *(Re: another photo)* Let's
get back to this one.

LARS: Thank you sir. Thank you.

MAN: But surely there must've been some sign back
then...something to indicate her dire predicament
now. Some germ of her terrible future captured in the
innocuous pixels of her past. *(Re: another photo)* Delete.

LARS: That one wasn't my fault, sir.

MAN: You, sitting here, and this forlorn little girl on her cold metal swing. *(Re another picture)* Delete.

LARS: She moved, I swear to god sir, she's doing it to get me in trouble.

MAN: Studying this girl on her swing, thinking, during my lunch, thinking—Is her potential already spent, already gone? Where will life take her, this lost little girl, when she jumps off that cold metal metal swing. Will it bring her here, to me, as it did with you… *(He shuffles idly through more photos.)* So often, you see, we grow away from ourselves, and yet deep down, deep down we remain exactly the same.
Isn't that right, Lars?

LARS: Regrettably so, sir.

MAN: The "before" and "after" that simply contributes to the condensed cloud of confusion we call identity. *(Returning camera, measure of disgust)* Delete all these.

LARS: Look, I know she's not inherently photogenic like us—seeing as where she comes from—but I swear on my mother's eyes you'll find the last one of great interest.

(LARS offers MAN the camera. MAN refuses.)

MAN: Not interested. No. What I'd like is for our guest to paint an honest portrait for us. And tell me who we have the pleasure of welcoming today. *(Turns to WOMAN)* Is it the forgotten young girl from the swings, or some trespassing stranger who has stolen your past and come here now to claim your husband.

WOMAN: There is no husband. I keep telling you that.

MAN: No. Of course not. Forgive me. Must be my mistake. The astigmatic error of my ways blurring everything together like that. *(Barking)* Lars!

LARS: Sir?

MAN: Schedule me an appointment with the Dr.
Walters right away.

LARS: Done, sir!

MAN: Maybe this way I'll be able to see through all the
bullshit better.

(LARS *and* MAN *laugh.*)

MAN: *(Sobering)* O K, now what do you say we start
from the top again. And this time try to paint a better
picture for us, make it a bit more... interesting. Alright?
(Pause) Why are you here?

(Silence)

MAN: *(Deliberate)* WHY THE FUCK ARE YOU HERE?!

(Silence)

WOMAN: I came to check up on my... *(Studied pause)*

MAN: Yes?

WOMAN: ...husband.

MAN: Husband?

WOMAN: *(Challenging)* Yes. Isn't that what you wanted
me to say? Thought would be so interesting...?

MAN: Think you're clever, don't you. Hey Lars, I think
we got us a clever one here.

LARS: That's too bad, sir.

MAN: You think this is all some big joke. Just change a
few words around and everything's all fixed. Doesn't
work that way. Not here. Not with me. For your
information I don't like scrabble. And I hate fuckin
crossword puzzles. If you say it—you've got to really
mean it. Words have to carry some currency with me.
Get that. I'm doing you a favor here. Granting you this
private audience. Helping you look for someone you

love. You think I like my job here...? Separating the chaff from the wheat. Ascertaining who is and isn't wanted by the State? I've gone and put myself out here... And this is how you chose to thank me. Tsk. Tsk. Tsk.

WOMAN: *(Urgent)* Then why don't you believe me? Why do you refuse to believe me when I tell you he's my brother.

MAN: *(Expansive)* Sometimes a person goes wandering in the woods. Gets lost. It's hardly ever deliberate. Most often when a person gets lost, it's by accident... don't you agree?

WOMAN: I don't understand.

MAN: To me you seem very lost, utterly confused. Like a girl in need of some good...guidance. A woman who's strayed too far from her home.

WOMAN: But there's no reason for me to lie like this. I'm here legally. Why would I lie to you?

MAN: Maybe you want to protect him, mmmm?

WOMAN: From what? Protect him from what?

MAN: You tell us...sister.

WOMAN: But what's he done? I don't even know what he's done.

MAN: It's better that way. For you. For him. These are unfriendly times with unfriendly laws. Doubts darken quickly. People vanish easily. *(Beat)* Now what makes you so sure we know where he is?

WOMAN: They told me...they told me he was brought here.

MAN: They...? Again with they. Who is this they...?

WOMAN: I can't...remember.

MAN: No...you wouldn't.

WOMAN: *(Small voice)* I'm sorry

MAN: *(Turning, abrupt)* You can go. Thank you.

WOMAN: Excuse me...?

MAN: How much patience do you think I have? Lars, please show this woman out.

WOMAN: But I was told—

MAN: What? What were you told?

WOMAN: You told me...

MAN: ...that you'd be allowed to see him. *(Coyly)* Well, you did. You did see him. Don't you remember? As I far as I can recall, in my book, you even shared a cigarette or two. Maybe you just don't remember, eh? A ticklish matter this business with memory. Lars, do you by chance recall having brought the prisoner in?

LARS: *(Playing along)* Most certainly sir.

MAN: And did he seem to know this lady?

LARS: There was a strong attraction there.

MAN: Brother and sister...?

LARS: *(Perversely)* More like husband and wife.

WOMAN: *(Protesting)* But I told you. I am his sister. Why do you keep doing this? What do you want from me?

MAN: Are you still here?

WOMAN: You promised. You said...

MAN: I have no idea what you're talking about. *(Beat)* Cold...?

WOMAN: Excuse me?

MAN: You look cold. Should I shut the window?

WOMAN: Whatever.

MAN: Open or closed?

WOMAN: I don't care. My brother...

MAN: It's important to make a choice. You get no points here for being polite with me. Right or wrong it's important that you claim a choice. Open or closed?

WOMAN: Closed.

(MAN *stands to shut window.*)

MAN: *(Testing)* Closed...?

(*Afraid she gave the wrong answer,* WOMAN *quickly changes her mind.*)

WOMAN: No, open.

MAN: *(Still testing)* Open?

WOMAN: It doesn't matter.

MAN: I see....

WOMAN: *(More unsure)* Really. I don't care. I don't fuckin care anymore!!

(MAN *sits back down. Leaves window open. Pause*)

MAN: *(Calm and menacing)* Is that so...? You don't care anymore. You really don't fuckin care.

(*Silence*)

WOMAN: Look, I'm sorry. Please...please forgive me. My brother. I beg you. I didn't mean to lose my temper.

MAN: *(Overlapping)* Lars... you hear that? This lady doesn't fuckin care anymore.

WOMAN: Why won't you let me see him.

MAN: *(With measured relish)* Fuckin...fuckin...fuckin... fuckin...

WOMAN: Please... I just want to make sure he's alright.

MAN: I'd love to, more than anything, believe me I'd love to make you happy. Sister, wife...*hermana, esposa...*

makes little difference to me. You have to believe
that. But I really don't think he's here. At least not
that I fuckin know of. Then again I may be fuckin
wrong. Here at the agency we try and make a point of
never being too proud to admit our mistakes. Now if
someone told you otherwise—someone with a definite
name, a listed address, has informed you otherwise—
perhaps they know something I don't. Perhaps I may
be wrong after all. I'm not infallible you know. All you
have to do is... convince me.

WOMAN: *(Defeated, small voice)* It was a colleague...from
work...he did mention something...

MAN: Lars.

LARS: Sir...?

MAN: Did you say something?

LARS: No sir.

MAN: *(Picks up binoculars, looks at birds)* I thought I
heard something. Must be those birds again. This new
feeder is really too much. All day, from dawn to dusk,
they don't stop coming...eating and chirping all day
long—migrating here, migrating there—whispering
small bright secrets as they go. I'm thinking of
installing a bird bath next. So I can see the little lovelies
clean themselves after they eat. What do you say
Lars...? Think there's room to hang a little bath on the
balcony?

WOMAN: *(Louder, more distinct)* A colleague... at work.
He said my brother was here.

MAN: A colleague?

WOMAN: *(Evasive)* But vaguely... only vaguely...it was
just a thought...he didn't really know. Said he can't
be sure but it might be worth looking into, that's all,
really...

MAN: Name.

WOMAN: I don't want to get anyone in trouble. I promised not to—

MAN: *(Sharp)* NAME!

WOMAN: *(Reluctantly)* It might have been Wolinsky, something to that effect.

MAN: Wolinsky...is that Jewish?

WOMAN: I'm not sure.

MAN: How do you spell it?

WOMAN: Like it sounds, I think.

MAN: What it sounds like is a troublemaker to me. Name ring a bell with you Lars?

LARS: *(Trying it on)* WO-LINSKY...Wolinsky...I knew a certain Wolansky once.

MAN: What happened to him?

LARS: Arrested years ago. Probably out on parole by now.

MAN: Think it might be the same man?

LARS: Why not? Sounds close enough.

MAN: Schedule an interview with him.

LARS: Right away, sir.

WOMAN: But—

MAN: *(Cutting her off)* Don't worry. Nothing will happen to him. Just want to broach a few simple questions to this Wolansky of yours...

WOMAN: *(Correcting him)* Wolinsky.

MAN: Wolinksy, Wolansky—now you say he said you might be able to find him here...your brother.

WOMAN: Yes. That's right.

MAN: You realize we have a lot of people here? Quite difficult to sort them out. In their creased gray uniforms, heads all shorn, babbling away in their strange native tongue, they all start to look alike after a while...men, women...boys, girls...

WOMAN: Isn't there some way to check...a list or something?

MAN: A list..? (*Mocking, histrionic, slaps his head*) Lars could you bring me that list at once!!

(LARS *doesn't move, emits a chuckles.* MAN *also laughs.*)

MAN: No, no...you're going to have to do a lot better than that. If you want to see this man you call your brother, you'll have to provide us with an impeccably accurate and detailed description.

WOMAN: I'm not sure I know exactly how to...

MAN: (*Impatient*)

Describe him!

WOMAN: Where... I don't know...where to start....

MAN: (*Overlapping*) Tall.

(*Pause*)

MAN: Is he tall?

WOMAN: Average.

MAN: Average. Mmmm...like me? (*He stands.*)

WOMAN: No.

MAN: No...?

WOMAN: More like him.

(WOMAN *gestures at* LARS. *He stands.*)

MAN: (*To* LARS) Are you writing that down?

LARS: (*Somewhat pleased*) More like me.

MAN: Aren't you lucky? *(To* WOMAN*)* What color hair...?

WOMAN: Brown...no, auburn.

MAN: Like him? *(He gestures at* LARS.*)*

WOMAN: No like you.

MAN: *(To* LARS*)* You get that.

LARS: *(Somewhat deflated)* Dark auburn. Not at all like me.

MAN: Eyes...?

WOMAN: I have to think.

MAN: Don't you know your own brother's eyes?

WOMAN: It's complicated.

MAN: Really. Can't be that hard. *(Covering his eyes, rapidly)* Lars, what color are my eyes?

LARS: *(Responding blindly)* Brown, sir.

MAN: See that... And we're not even brothers. Are we Lars? *(Lars laughs)* Hey Lars, what do you think about you and I becoming brothers...?

*(*MAN *and* LARS *laugh harder.)*

MAN: Would you like that? I'd have to be the older one of course, beat the living daylights out of you all over again... What do you say? You up for getting the shit kicked out of you? Your fingers crushed under shiny brotherly boots? *(To* WOMAN*)* Did your so-called brother ever lay a hand on you? Did he ever pinch you in your crib when the folks weren't looking. Spit on your food at dinner time...? He is older isn't he, your brother?

WOMAN: Blue.

MAN: What's that?

WOMAN: His eyes. Before... you asked me...

MAN: *(Overlapping, astonished)* Blue...?

WOMAN: When he's wearing blue.

MAN: *(To* LARS*)* Did you follow that?

WOMAN: *(Inserting)* Otherwise green.

LARS: Green eyes. Except when wearing blue.

MAN: Anything else?

(WOMAN *tries to think. Grows agitated. Shakes her head pensively)*

MAN: *(Clipped)* No distinguishing features? Marks? Manner of speech. Attitude when sitting. Standing. Walking. The way he smiles, frowns, answers the phone. Drinks his coffee. Brushes his teeth. Ties his shoes. Knots his tie. Clips his nails. Cuts his hair. Shaves his face. *(Man brushes her face with his fingers.)* Complexion... Yes, how is his complexion?

WOMAN: You're getting me all confused here.

MAN: But I'm only trying to help you.

WOMAN: Yes...I know.

MAN: Look after your best interests.

WOMAN: I know...yes.

MAN: *(Rushed, breathless)* But perhaps I'm going too fast for you. Am I going too fast? I could always slow down, you know. But let me assure you that slowing down is just a waste of time when there's so much going on in the world today. That's why we must always be one step ahead of ourselves. And that goes for everyone...even Lars.

LARS: Especially Lars, sir.

MAN: When you think of all the thoughts, words, orbiting up there in your head, at the same time, it's amazing anything coherent ever gets said.

LARS: Or understood.

(MAN *gives him a scathing look.*)

MAN: For instance, right now, right now I'm beginning to have a thought...

LARS: Oooo... I'd love to hear it sir.

MAN: Granted, at this point it's still quite young and formative.

LARS: I'm sure it's brilliant.

MAN: But I can feel it starting to take shape. To assert itself with a specific language and grammar like some primordial gas trying to vainly coalesce in the middle of space. Or...or like when you recognize the melody of a song before recalling its name, or the words, and you feel like you know something before you even know it. This is where my thought is now residing, parked in this strange prophetic limbo, which to be perfectly honest, is starting to make me exceedingly lonely. This constant anticipation of language. What if it never comes? The words? What will happen to my orphaned thought then?

(LARS *shrugs.*)

MAN: If only I could maintain a vigil of silence like you, that'd be great. But that won't work for me. I'm much more needy. My thought needs an audience, a witness to coax it into life.

LARS: I'll be your audience.

MAN: You don't count.

LARS: What about her?

MAN: Depends.

WOMAN: I don't mind.

MAN: Are you sure…? I'm not an easy man to please. Far from agreeable, my thoughts are rarely ingratiating.

WOMAN: I don't care.

MAN: When you first came in and sat down… What was your first impression of me. Before any words were thought or spoken? Waiting for the questioning to begin. Did you think me kind, sympathetic…? Or did you already isolate that flash of cruelty in my eyes.

WOMAN: I wanted to like you.

MAN: Really?

WOMAN: It was in my best interest to like you.

MAN: But I disabused you of that soon enough.

WOMAN: You kept adjusting your tie. Like it was a noose around your neck, you kept fidgeting with it while you were feeding the birds. And I couldn't help but think what is he like in the morning, before he opens the door to his office, when he just wakes up from his dream? Is there some sacred, unguarded moment of innocence before the day kicks in and the tie gets knotted. Do you at some point meet your gaze in the mirror with a vague, perhaps even benevolent, approval. Or is it all just another opportunity to rehearse the contempt you harbor for the world at large.

MAN: Wow! You don't talk much, do you—but when you do it's even more eloquent than your silence.

LARS: Enviable sir, quite enviable.

MAN: And this from someone who's bi—

LARS: *(Excited, aroused)* Oooo!

MAN: —lingual that is.

LARS: *(Dejected)* Oh...

MAN: Coming from someone like that, the effort is even more admirable and impressive.

LARS: *(Jotting)* Bi-lingual.

MAN: I mean it's a wonder you can speak at all, given your predicament. One language always vying with the other for supremacy. English thoughts spying on Spanish thoughts and vice versa.

WOMAN: That's not what it feels like to me.

MAN: Granted I speak English, only English, a mother tongue rife with Oedipal tendencies, and even so my thoughts are not always the most cogent or clear, but still, still I...I...I... *(He pauses. As if struck by a sudden bout of amnesia. Like an actor forgetting his lines...)*

LARS: Sir...?

MAN: Don't interrupt!! I... Fuck I...can't believe it, I forgot...

LARS: That's what happens when you stop to explain sir.

MAN: Shit!

LARS: Exposition is evil.

MAN: It was really important too.

LARS: I'm sure it was. Coming from you how can it not be.

MAN: Fuck me!

LARS: It will come back.

If it's important it will...

MAN: *(Overlapping)* That's what they always say, but it's not true. Is it? IS IT?!!!

(WOMAN looks down.)

MAN: You try to say the right thing, search for the right word, rescue it form oblivion, but when it goes, it's gone for good. Consigned to that great landfill of words. Never to be seen or heard from again. And all you're left with is this clawing sense of urgency. As if you lost some essential part of yourself. And you don't even know what that part is.

WOMAN: I'm sorry.

MAN: You should be. It's all your fault! Sequestered behind your bilingual silence, urging me to talk, making me forget...

WOMAN: You can't blame me for that.

MAN: Why not? WHY NOT?

WOMAN: I didn't do anything...I was just...

MAN: Being your silent insolent self?! The way you just sit there, so proud and insular, translating everything I say into that Spanish in your head... That won't do around here.

LARS: No it won't.

MAN: Look. I'm not asking you to do anything unreasonable.

LARS: Fuck no.

MAN: I just want you to show a little spirit of cooperation. If we're going to help locate your... brother, it'd be much better if you could think in English. Describe him in English. Is that too much to ask for? I don't think so. Is it?

LARS: Don't look at me.

(Another planes passes, filling room with its roar.)

(Silence)

(MAN *returns to desk.)*

MAN: Okay, okay. So how about this. How about this: You've just called the restaurant. It's Friday night and the place is really packed. *(He punches some numbers into desk phone.)* The maitre'd answers. You ask him to help locate your...

WOMAN: Brother..?

MAN: Yes... It's urgent that you get a hold of him. For all you know his life my depend on it. But first you need to describe him. The maitre'd asks you to tell him what he looks like—What would you say?

WOMAN: I...

MAN: Remember. He is your brother after all...

WOMAN: Yes.

MAN: And this is a real emergency. No more of this academic bullshit, yes?

(WOMAN nods. MAN shoves phone at her.)

MAN: Ask for him. Go on. Page your brother. *(Snide)* Unless, of course, you think he might be washing dishes in the kitchen...

(WOMAN looks at phone. Motionless, angry)

MAN: Come on. The maitre'd is waiting. If you don't pick up, he'll hang up on you. Better hurry.

(WOMAN finally picks it up. Looks puzzled. Turns to MAN.)

MAN: Something wrong...?

WOMAN: There's someone there.

MAN: Of course there is. *(Mock, vicious)* What did you think?

WOMAN: Who is it...what number did you dial?

MAN: *(Motioning to phone)* He's waiting.

WOMAN: What should I say?

MAN: Describe your brother. Maybe he'll be found.

(WOMAN begins talking into phone. MAN chimes in the background. LARS, as ever, prepares to take notes.)

WOMAN: He...

MAN: Describe him accurately...unsparingly...fully.

WOMAN: *(Haltingly into phone)* He...

(Pause)

MAN: Yes...?

WOMAN: ...is...

MAN: *(Overlapping)* Ethnic?

WOMAN: *(Simultaneous with above)* ...generous and kind.

MAN: That's not a good description.

WOMAN: He is...

MAN: *(Again overlapping)* Ethnic?

WOMAN: ...good at telling jokes.

MAN: You're still skirting the issue.

WOMAN: Very...

MAN: *(Through his teeth)* ETHNIC.

WOMAN: ...charming but modest.

MAN: They'll need more than that you know.

WOMAN: It's the best I can do.

MAN: That's how you'd describe him?

WOMAN: For now, yes. I couldn't think of anything else.

MAN: You should've told them what they wanted to hear.

WOMAN: I told you I'm not very good at this.

MAN: Then you should've listened to me.

(WOMAN gestures for MAN to wait a moment, talks briefly into phone.)

WOMAN: *(Into phone)* Hello...? Yes, yes...I understand. *(She lowers phone.)*

MAN: What did they say?

WOMAN: Said he'll need more than that...

MAN: What did I tell you.

WOMAN: But he's willing to give the place a quick look around.

MAN: Good. Then your lucky. *(Beat)* You on hold?

WOMAN: I....

MAN: *(Cutting off)* Mind...? *(He takes phone out of her hand. Punches a button that puts it on speaker.)*

(In the background, barely audible from the speakerphone, a radio station issues the weather report for the day—bright and cheery with a slim chance of rain.)

MAN: What concerns me is the weather in here, inside this room. Not in Ciudad Juarez or Tijuana or Mexico City. But here in the comfortable borders of this room. *(He lowers the volume further. Turns to face WOMAN.)*

MAN: Now I suggest you use this time wisely...try and come up with something a little more persuasive for once...a description that has some merit to it... something they can actually go to work with....

WOMAN: But what else can I say? I told you I don't have much experience at this. I mean how do you go about describing someone's looks. Stubborn eyes... Soft mouth... That doesn't really paint a picture, does it?

MAN: It might. It might. All depends on how it's done. Manner with which it's...executed. You, for example, could be described using only two words: Beautiful and...exotic. Other women, no doubt, would demand a more rigorous rendering. *(Suddenly turning to LARS)* Lars, who was that lovely lady you told me about the other day...

LARS: Turns out, sir, she wasn't exactly a lady.

MAN: Not too disappointed, I hope.

LARS: On the contrary.

(LARS and MAN both giggle.)

MAN: Please, describe her to our guest the way you described her to me. *(He offers LARS his binoculars.)* Left quite a vivid impression as I recall.

LARS: Very well, sir... *(He takes binoculars. Trains them on WOMAN but seems to be having a hard time getting started.)*

LARS: I...

MAN: Having trouble...?

LARS: I can't explain it but....

MAN: You already forget...?

LARS: No sir.

(MAN approaches LARS, briefly regards binoculars, before flipping them around so that they now magnify instead of diminish.

MAN: Here. Better...?

LARS: Much. Much.

MAN: Please begin.

(Again LARS trains binoculars on WOMAN. Begins to circle her. Watching her seated there from various vantage points in the room—all the while offering his description.)

LARS: On her feet she wore temptingly small shoes...

MAN: Excellent. Yes... *(He lights a cigarette. Throws feet on desk. Smokes luxuriously as he listens.)* Start at the bottom and work your way up.

LARS: *(Looking at WOMAN through binoculars)* ...she wore temptingly small shoes, and when she sat it was on a pair of ripe fleshy thighs that were backed by a pair of fair but firm buttocks. Her waist was slender like the neck of a bottle. Her neck like a delicate vase displayed the bright rosy lips, always full and petulant. *(He briefly lowers binoculars to address* MAN.*)* But all this— as I've already told you and you already know—had naturally failed to compete—or even hold a candle to—her languishing dark Spanish eyes *(again picks up binoculars, studies Woman, but as before has trouble continuing)* Eyes...eyes...

(Pause)

MAN: *(Aroused)* Go on. For chrissakes don't stop now.

LARS flips binoculars about, smiles, continues.)

LARS: ...eyes sparkling and beaming with an inward lascivious fire, keen, searching eyes that were shaded by a curtain of long silken lashes... *(Still viewing* WOMAN *through binoculars, he approaches close enough to touch her hair)* ...And then of course there was her hair... living hair that sprayed in a profusion of ringlets over her neck and shoulders... *(His hand drops as if to caress her breasts while she sits stock still)* ...then down onto a pair of monumental mammaries more beautiful and mysterious even than the moons of Jupiter. Yes, and even then, at that moment, I knew she would always be more than a memory for me...much much more. But to her I meant nothing. Less than nothing. Because, you see, as it turns out she was a common garden whore...a prostitute of first degree. And I miss her terribly. *(He drops the binoculars.)*

*(*MAN *puts out cigarette. Coughs with finality. Breaking the spell)*

MAN: *(To* WOMAN*)* There...see what I mean? There you have it in a nutshell. The inestimable power of description. How it affects one's heart and loins all in one.

WOMAN: *(Defiant)* But...I still don't know what she looks like.

MAN: Don't you...?

WOMAN: I'm afraid not.

MAN: You trying to be difficult?

WOMAN: Of course not.

MAN: Well what about a public gathering...a company picnic?... Are you saying you wouldn't be able to pick her out reading in the public library? Walking down a busy street. At your favorite cousin's wedding? Is that what I'm hearing you say?

WOMAN: Not from what I've just heard, no... I'd have to first see a picture of some sort.

MAN: What about a crowd of men? Could you find this woman there? Amidst a crowd of men...?

WOMAN: A crowd of men...well, yes, that would be different now wouldn't it?

MAN: Unfortunately, though, there's only two of us here...that is men—Lars and myself. And two, as we all know, only counts as company, never a crowd. Now if your brother was here...yes, if your brother was here, with us, things would of course be very different. Wouldn't they? Wouldn't they?! We'd have us a nice little crowd then, wouldn't we...? Not a crowded crowd...just a nice crowd. The way I like it. So please help us...make an effort. Your brother...what does he look like? Does he look at all like you? Would a stranger make some connection between you and him on the street...? Come on...say something. Feel free to chime in. Surely you must've shared some childhood memories together—you and your beloved brother? What was the name of your favorite ice cream man? The dog who got run over. The time you and your brother had a fight and you stuck a needle in the carpet

waiting all afternoon for him to step on it. Hello?
...Anything ring a bell here...? *(Pause)* Hello, is anyone
there?

LARS: *(Reflective, low)* Now that you mention it, I do
remember stepping on a needle once, but I always
thought...

MAN: *(Exploding)* Not you, fuckpig!! Haven't you
talked enough for one day?!

LARS: Sorry sir.

MAN: *(To* WOMAN, *sweetly)* Now...where were we?

WOMAN: They've put me on hold. *(Motioning to
speakerphone)* I'm still on hold.

MAN: Well...there's always hope, isn't there?

WOMAN: That's why I came.

MAN: *(Interjecting)* Yes....

WOMAN: *(Overlapping)* Why I'm here.

MAN: I understand.

WOMAN: I...need your help. Everyone warned me
against coming here. Said it would be pointless to deal
with you. That in the end it would only work against
me...

MAN: But you decided to come down anyway. How
noble.

WOMAN: Please...please help me.

MAN: Have you ever stopped to listen to yourself...
how desperate you sound?

WOMAN: I'm sorry.

MAN: *(Overriding)* It's not very attractive, you know, no
one likes needy people.

WOMAN: I said I was sorry.

MAN: You're not the only one with a story to tell. My great-grandparents were potato-starved Irish who jumped off the boat at Ellis Island. Lars' were filthy Italian immigrants that never learned the language of the land.

LARS: That's...not exactly true, sir.

MAN: Oh really...?

LARS: They had, in fact, memorized one poem.

MAN: In English?...

LARS: I beleive it was inscribed on the Statue of Liberty

MAN: You never told me this.

(LARS *stands stiffly, lifts an arm up to emulate Statue of Liberty. And begins reciting the poem.*)

LARS: *The New Colosus:*
Give me your tired, your poor,
Your huddled masses yearning to breathe free
The wretched refuse of your teeming shores
Send these, the homeless, tempest- tost to me.
I lift my lamp beside the golden door!
(*He lowers his arm. Curtsies. Then adds as afterthought:*) by Emma Lazarus

MAN: *(Standing)* Bravo! Bravo!

LARS: Thank you sir.

MAN: *(To* WOMAN*)* See...see what I mean...everyone's had a hard time of it. Tired and poor. Homeless and tempest-tost. His ancestors. Mine. They all worked so hard and suffered even harder. Entire lives were sacrificed. Generations lost. My grandparents for my parents, my parents for me—and you...yes, you for your brother. That's what's it all about. Progress. What we're all striving so hard to achieve. The ancestral food chain of progenitor and offspring.

WOMAN: But you still haven't told me what you want.

MAN: *(Ignoring her)* Tell me something, when was the last time you had a close look at the Statue of Liberty... at her face. I mean a real careful look at her cold metallic countenance. If you do you'll see she isn't exactly smiling. *(He touches her lips.)* No, not even the smallest trace of a smile. On the contrary, those lips have been hammered into a taut and serious and.... uncompromising expression. *(Slight pause)* What goes on here is of utmost gravity... importance. To change your identity. Your home. Not every caterpillar is permitted to become a beautiful butterfly.

WOMAN: Just tell me what you want. Please. What exactly do you want from me?!

(MAN smiles.)

MAN: Mmmm...what I want, yes, what I want.... well, perhaps we're going about this all wrong. What do you think? Should we start all over...? Eh? Pretend this is a real interview. A job interview. And you are here trying to impress me. You are trying to impress me I hope?

(WOMAN nods meekly.)

MAN: Good. Very good. Now you're probably thinking what does he have in mind? Where's he taking all this. Well, aren't you? An interview of what sort... For what? ...you might ask. What exactly is the putative nature of this interview? The compass of this job? It's precise needs and qualifications? *(Beat)* Well, go on. Ask me. Give it a shot. What does this job entail? Ask me. Where does it all lead to?

WOMAN: I...

MAN: *(Dramatically innocent)* You'd like to ask me something?

WOMAN: *(Defeated)* Yes.

MAN: About this job...?

(WOMAN *nods.*)

MAN: Funny... Had a feeling it might be something like that. Isn't that funny?

(WOMAN *smiles wanly.*)

MAN: Lars, how many other applicants do we have lined up for today?

LARS: Quite a handful, sir.

MAN: And how are we on time?

LARS: Running out, sir. Always running out.

MAN: *(To* WOMAN*)* I'm sorry. You were saying...

WOMAN: This job...

MAN: Go on. I'm listening.

WOMAN: What precisely would this job entail?

MAN: Interested...?

WOMAN: That's why I'm here...yes.

MAN: Excellent. Because you see I'm in desperate need of a good nanny. Don't look so shocked. Please. It's not for me. My children. Why does that amaze you so much? That I have children, a family... Why does that surprise you to such a great degree? I also have a dog if you must know. Portuguese water dog, supposed to be expert divers, born with a special tail that helps them navigate the currents. But want to know what truly distinguishes these fine creatures from the rest of their kind....? It's what they do on their off-season, when the fishing is low and they're carefully trained to become part-time sheep dog. Amazing isn't it? What do you do on your off-season? Do you lactate, micturate, defecate...? Are you well versed in infant C P R as well as the Heimlich maneuver? What exactly, if I may ask, do you do—period?

(*Pause*)

WOMAN: I'm a schoolteacher.

MAN: So you'd be good with discipline. Drawing
the line. Establishing the necessary boundaries. See,
my kids are in dire need of discipline. Aren't we all?
Impossible brats. Buy them expensive toys, they play
with pots and pans. Lars has met them, haven't you
Lars? Even had the pleasure of babysitting on the odd
night when we found ourselves in a pinch. A little
prompting and I'm sure he'll be happy to testify to the
difficult nature of the task.

LARS: *(Almost under his breath)* Little shits...always
making a goddamn mess...

(MAN coughs sharply as warning.)

LARS: *(Punches fist into palm)* Just once...just once, I'd
like to teach 'em the real meaning of the word behave.

MAN: *(Cautioning)* Lars...

LARS: I meant mine sir. Mine are filthy...stinking...turds
by comparison to yours.

MAN: No need to go overboard, Lars.

LARS: Just stating the facts, sir.

MAN: *(Overlapping)* Flattery will only get you so far. *(an
afterthought)* Although usually, I admit, that's quite far
enough. *(Beat)* Do you enjoy working for me, Lars...?

(LARS looks up.)

MAN: Do you ever regret being in my employ?

LARS: No, never sir.

MAN: Even when I sometimes bark at you?

LARS: When you do, I deserve it.

MAN: Or lose my temper for no obvious reason...?

LARS: Wouldn't have it any other way, sir.

MAN: *(To* WOMAN, *exultant)* See...that's the kind of worker I'm looking for. Those are the kind of shoes I need filled. Think you are up for it? All the intricacies and subtlety it involves?

WOMAN: I...could give it...a try. But...

MAN: *(Jumping in)* Something not to your liking? Your taste?

WOMAN: No...I...

MAN: *(Overriding, peremptory)* Lars, I thought you said her papers were all in order?

LARS: They appeared to be, sir, but—

MAN: *(Overlapping)* Couldn't have an official like me involved in a mess like that.

LARS: No sir.

MAN: Never know when these things'll catch up with you. *(Beat)* So what seems to be the problem here? Don't you want to work for me?

WOMAN: It's not that...

MAN: You sound a bit tentative. Somewhat apprehensive. Or are you just being prudent? You look like a prudent person...very thoughtful, calculating, and I don't necessarily mean that in the bad sense of the word. Yes, well what do you say about a little pop quiz...something to really test your mettle...see what you're really made of. Are you paying attention? It's important that you listen to everything I have to say. Absorb each word as I speak it. Assuming, that is, you're really serious about this job to begin with.

WOMAN: And...my brother? What does all this have to do with him? Have you entirely forgotten about my brother?

(MAN stares at WOMAN. Annoyed at the interruption)

MAN: What do you think?

(MAN *turns up volume on speakerphone. They are still on hold. Pouring out the speakerphone is a traffic report being aired over the radio station on the other end. A terrible accident. Long delays*)

MAN: Is that him? Does that sound like him?

WOMAN: No.

MAN: Good. Means they're probably still out there looking.

WOMAN: Or maybe they forgot. Got busy and forgot they put me on hold.

MAN: They wouldn't forget. I know that restaurant. Personal friends with the manager there. Wife and I... we're what you'd call regulars. Their most regular regulars in fact. Never fucked up an order the whole time we've gone there. No matter how complicated or busy. Must have something to do with the kind of people they hire...the kind of English they speak. Entre nous... place has the best Tunisian eggplant appetizer I can think of...which is not to say that I wouldn't give the most glowing report to their Tuscan Bean soup... or take a cut in pay to simply have another taste of their incomparable Javanese vegetable salad...but I'm afraid I'm allowing my appetite to get the best of me... (*He reaches across desk to turn up volume on speakerphone.*) You mind...?

(*Traffic report narrating the accident fades.*)

MAN: I hate those things. Fuckin accidents! Greatest fear is that I'll be stuck cursing in traffic somewhere listening to that shit, when all at once I realize that the accident they're broadcasting actually involves someone I know or love. But who fuckin cares...right? We're here—and all those assholes are out there. So pay close attention. If you want the job listen to what

I'm putting out and make sure to pick up on it. *(Beat)*
It's, yes, yet another Friday night. And we're out on the
town—me and the Mrs—a nice dinner, then a movie.
You are home with Jane and Michael. Jane is in the
bath, but Michael is in the kitchen. All of a sudden you
hear Michael scream. What do you do?

WOMAN: I'm still not sure what all this has to do with...

MAN: *(Urgent)* What do you do? This is an emergency
for Chrissake. No time to fret about your brother.

WOMAN: *(Perfunctorily)* First I pick Jane out of the tub,
then rush over to the kitchen to see what's happened
with Michael.

MAN: Very good. Excellent. Always remove the child
from water. Never leave them unattended. Then what?

WOMAN: I search the fridge door for the number of the
restaurant you left me.

MAN: Go on. Elaborate.

WOMAN: I call and ask for you or your wife.

MAN: What if we don't have reservations...

WOMAN: Excuse me?

MAN: Reservations...what if we neglected to make any.

WOMAN: Then I describe you to the maitre'd.

MAN: *(Triumphant, sharing this with* LARS*)* You describe
us...?

WOMAN: That's right.

MAN: And what do you say? What exactly... do you
say? Your description. What are the words you choose
to describe us with?

WOMAN: I'm sorry...but the phone...I think.

MAN: What?

(WOMAN *leans closer to speakerphone on desk.*)

WOMAN: Listen...

(LARS and MAN do.)

WOMAN: I think there's someone there. They're back. I think they're back. *(She reaches for phone.)* Can I...?

(He motions for WOMAN to pick up the receiver.)

MAN: It's your dime...metaphorically speaking that is.

(WOMAN picks up phone. It goes off speaker.)

WOMAN: *(Into phone)* Hello? Hello...?

(But as WOMAN begins to talk—another plane passes overhead, drowning out her conversation.)

(Then silence)

(WOMAN now stares at phone in her hand, almost in disbelief.)

MAN: *(Upbeat)* So...about the job? Think you got it? Passed the test..? You know...not getting hired, is just like getting fired.

WOMAN: *(Half-stunned, slow)* They couldn't find him.

MAN: Doesn't mean he wasn't there, you know.

WOMAN: Said my description wasn't...adequate.

MAN: I told you not to get your hopes up. *(To LARS)* Didn't I tell her...?

(LARS acquiesces, nods grandly.)

WOMAN: They hung up. There was a loud noise and then we got disconnected.

MAN: Want me to call again?

(WOMAN stares sightlessly ahead.)

MAN: *(Bouyant)* It's no problem. Really. *(He punches redial button.)* Just press redial. And...

(Busy signal sounds over the speaker)

MAN: We'll try again later, don't look so tragic...

WOMAN: But you should've heard it...that noise...and then we got disconnected.

MAN: Probably nothing. Someone dropping dishes in the kitchen. That's all.

WOMAN: No. It sounded a lot more...sinister than that. Like..like...

MAN: Some sort of serious accident?

WOMAN: Yes...yes. How did you know?

MAN: Perhaps if next time you provide them with a better description...you'll get better results. Perhaps next time you should try telling them it's your husband you're looking for, and see what kind of answer they come up with.

WOMAN: But he isn't...

MAN: Is...isn't.... Did you know that in the Bible (yes, now and then I do read the Bible) ...did you know that when Abraham went down into the land of Egypt, he'd convinced his wife to present herself as his sister although, in fact, they were just newly married. Have you any ideas as to why he'd do such a curious thing?

WOMAN: I...don't know.

MAN: No, you wouldn't. Why would you? *(He removes a key from around his neck. Dangles it before her, then reaches down to open one of the desk drawers, removes a black and heavy bible.)* Tell me something...yes, tell me. When was the last time you glanced at the good book? Dwelled over one of its many illuminating passages? Reviewed the Ten Commandments... in numerical order that is? Thou shall...thou shall not... Now there's a book that knows what it wants to say. A book brimming with exhilarating tales of exodus and hard-pressed immigrants trusting God to lead them into better lands. Better lives. Have you ever thought of reading the Bible? Well, perhaps you should give it some serious consideration. There's a lot to learn from it. Endless lessons, timeless parables. It's not for nothing that Christ died. He wanted you to read this book! There are things in there he wanted you to...well, be well-acquainted with. For example, why in heaven's sake would Abraham introduce his bride as his sister? Unless of course she was his sister as well as his wife... But I doubt that. Some taboos are even stronger than time itself. That's how they become such strong taboos. So tell me. About yourself? Your brother...? Abraham and his wife? What's exactly's going on here. Some scholars say that Abraham, a foreigner in a strange land, was afraid and concerned. Are you also concerned...?! Tell me what you're so concerned about?

WOMAN: Why are you doing all this...? Is it me? Because of who I am? Where I come from? What have I ever done to you...?

MAN: See, way the story goes is that Abraham's wife was such a knockout, he was afraid that other men, Egyptians mostly, would plot his death so they could take her from him. But if she was the sister... there would be no threat or competition...*capiche*? No harm or danger would come his way...at the expense, of course, of his beautiful wife's...shall we say...accessibility. *(Beat)* Now are you trying to make yourself accessible here? Are you trying to tell me that you're his sister so I'll sleep with you and save your husband? Is that what you're doing..?

WOMAN: But I'm not his wife...I'm his...

MAN: *(Cutting her off)* That's what they all say. Where's your wedding ring?

WOMAN: I told you...I told you everything...

MAN: You told me shit!! Are you willing to swear on this Bible? Are you willing to...

(MAN *shoves bible at* WOMAN.)

WOMAN: *(Overlapping)* Yes.

MAN: You are...?

(WOMAN *places her hand on bible.)*

WOMAN: I swear...

MAN: *(Overlapping)* You're willing to take God's oath, using my family bible, that you're...his sister.

WOMAN: *(Overlapping)* ...I swear that I'm his sister.

(Pause)

MAN: How dare you? How fuckin dare you exploit the Bible...my family's bible...for your shitty little means. *(He snatches the bible from her hands, spits on it, and polishes it with his shirt.)* Where in fucksname is your fear of God woman?!

WOMAN: *(Rising)* Can I please see him now?

MAN: You sit the fuck down! You hear me?! SIT THE FUCK DOWN!!

WOMAN: *(Sitting)* But I swore. On the bible...like you wanted me to...I...I...

MAN: That was between you and God. Has nothing to do with me. Understand?! Nothing! In this room it's just you and me. You and me.

(LARS *stands, moves forward to be included.)*

(Plane passes. Silence)

(LARS *sits.)*

WOMAN: Is he dead...? Is that it? Why you won't let me see him? You said I'd be able to see him. I don't understand why you're...

(MAN *throws an envelope across desk.)*

MAN: Here.

WOMAN: What is it?

MAN: Before I forget...he wanted you to have this.

WOMAN: So he was here. He was here.

MAN: Don't ask me why, but he wanted his wife to have this.

WOMAN: But I'm not...

MAN: Yeah, I know. But that's not what he said. He said you were his wife. Said you were definitely and categorically his wife.

WOMAN: Because you made him. You must've made him. Didn't you? Didn't you...?

MAN: Are we making you? Is anyone here twisting your arm? Exerting any pernicious pressure, undue influence...? Are we in any way, shape, or form, bending your mind against your will?

WOMAN: *(Softly)* No...

MAN: What?

WOMAN: *(Louder)* NO.

MAN: That's right. It's not how we do business here. We're not animals.

(MAN *and* LARS *straighten ties simultaneously.*)

MAN: Now aren't you going to open your little souvenir?

(WOMAN opens envelope cautiously, slowly, removes a scissored hank of hair from inside, studies it, returns it to envelope, looks up, fresh tears.

WOMAN: *(Cool and deliberate)* Dios mío! He's dead. Isn't he? You've killed him. You son-of-a-bitch! You've murdered my brother.

MAN: Now now, don't you think you're overreacting here... That's just some hair. Not an ear. Or finger.

Everyone here has their hair cut upon being admitted. It's simply standard sanitary procedure. Chances are he's still very much alive.... Isn't that so Lars?

LARS: Yes sir. In fact I think I saw him in the recreation room just the other day.

MAN: See... We're just having a little trouble locating his exact whereabouts. That's all.

(Long pause)

(WOMAN collects herself. Slowly rises)

WOMAN: I'd like to go. Can I please leave? Am I allowed to go? I'd like to go home please.

MAN: Of course. Of course. No one's holding you here. This isn't school. No waiting for the bell to ring...not here. You've been free to go from the start. Hasn't she Lars? Right from the word go.

(LARS opens door.)

MAN: Go on.

(No one moves.)

MAN: Can't say I blame you. It's hard to own responsibility for what we do. Who we are. You might walk out that door, but whatever you do, where ever you go, you are still trapped in your own head, caged by the poverty of your own thoughts. So how do you ever escape? Or do you...?

(WOMAN gathers her things, stands.)

MAN: For me, believe it or not, it's you. I get to talk to you. Find out everything about you and your dear beloved brother. That's what makes my life worthwhile. And why it hurts so much when you propagate your lies with such reckless abandon.

(WOMAN crosses to door, stops, and turns to face MAN.)

MAN: Ah, something on your mind...

WOMAN: I...

(Pause)

MAN: Some parting words...?

WOMAN: No...

MAN: How very disappointing. As a practicing schoolteacher, I was sure you'd glean some poignant lesson from all this. Distill some choice words, a meaningful message to make us all feel a shade or two better about ourselves. But I guess I was wrong.

WOMAN: *(Cold undertone)* May God have mercy on your soul.

MAN: You say something? Lars, someone say something?

LARS: Must be the birds, sir.

WOMAN: *(Through her teeth)* Vete al diablo.

MAN: Translation please!

LARS: I think sir, it means— "To hell with you!"

MAN: Really?

LARS: More or less, more or less.

MAN: *(Trying it out)* Vete al diablo.

LARS: Very good sir.

MAN: *(Glib, to* WOMAN*)* Now were you talking to me...? *(Points to* LARS*)* Or him?

WOMAN: Both of you. You'd think evolution would've rooted you're type out by now...but I guess not. Maybe you are the stronger ones. For now. But what does that mean...to be strong like you? What the fuck does that mean? Does it make you feel good? Important? What really separates you from me? Could it be the words that come from such a place of privilege? The pale skin into which you were accidentally born..? What makes you so different? Tell me, what do you do at the end of your day that's so special...? Go home and have a nice steak? Some coffee and dessert? Smoke a cigarette, then fuck your wife till you fall asleep...? *(Slight pause)* I hope to God you never have to go through what you've done to me or my brother. Because that's not the revenge I want for you. What would make me truly happy is that one day you'll comprehend what you've done...understand the depth of the suffering you've inflicted. Because right now, ignorant as you are, you're invincible. And the only justice or even hint of justice that exists, is that I'll never become like you or anything you stand for. That's the only true border that exists between us. The only border I vow never to cross.... *(She turns to go.)*

MAN: Just a minute please.

(WOMAN halts. Not turning. Almost out the door)

(MAN picks up phone, dials.)

WOMAN: *(Strong)* I thought you said I was free to go.

MAN: You are...it's your choice. Entirely your choice...

(WOMAN turns to face MAN.)

WOMAN: *(Suspicious)* But...?

MAN: No "buts" ...just wanted to keep you posted on the latest update. *(He points phone in her direction.)* Let you know it's ringing. Want to give it another try? Seems like I've somehow managed to get through at the restaurant.

WOMAN: What for? This another one of your games?

MAN: *(Into phone)* Yes...she's here, yes, but she seems a bit reluctant about approaching the phone. I see... Yes, I understand.

WOMAN: *(A glint of hope)* Is someone really there?

(Holding out phone to WOMAN)

MAN: See for yourself.

WOMAN: Haven't you had enough entertainment for one day?

MAN: They're all set to help you now. Apparently the place has really thinned out. Must've been that loud and eager theater crowd...you know, dine early, go catch an important show. No, they should have no trouble locating him now that the place is almost empty. All you have to do is slightly alter your description. Tell them that you're looking for...your husband.

WOMAN: My...my... (*She can't very well bring herself to say it.*)

MAN: So...what's the verdict? (*Wagging phone in front of her*) Yes...no...you need more time to think about it...? What do you want me to tell them?

WOMAN: You think this time they'll really be able to find him?

MAN: One way to find out. (*He continues to tempt her with the phone receiver.*)

(WOMAN *considers. Then re-enters room*)

(MAN *clears his throat.*)

MAN: One more thing.

(WOMAN *halts abruptly. Smiles sadly, knowingly*)

MAN: Seeing as you're already up and all, could you... please shut the window. (*Pause*) No hidden agenda here. I promise.

(WOMAN *slowly crosses room. Begins to close window*)

MAN: That's enough, thank you.

(WOMAN *returns to desk, holds her hand out for the phone.*)

(MAN *floats the phone within reach, but doesn't yet relinquish his hold on it.*)

MAN: You do realize what this means. *(Pause)* You do realize that perjury carries a very stiff penalty with it.

WOMAN: *(Somewhat confused)* Perjury...?

MAN: Lars was a witness when you took your oath. Weren't you, Lars?

LARS: That's right, sir.

MAN: He saw you swearing on the Bible...

LARS: Your family Bible, if I'm not mistaken sir. The Senora swore she was...his sister.

MAN: You take this phone now and tell 'em your his wife...well, it won't look so good.

WOMAN: I don't care.

MAN: What's the minimum time for perjury, Lars... three years?

LARS: Five, sir.

MAN: You hear that? Five years. Assuming you're not deported first.

WOMAN: *(Overlapping)* I said I don't care. Not if they can find him. Not as long as they can find him.

MAN: You sure you know what you're doing? *(He picks up the envelope with hair. Empties it on desk.)* I've heard nasty rumors about the help here.

WOMAN: Just hand me the phone.

(MAN deposits phone in WOMAN's hand. She hungrily speaks into it.)

WOMAN: *(Into phone)* Hello...? Yes, it's an emergency. I'm looking for...for my husband. Yes...I'll wait. Yes. Thank you, thank you.

MAN: Well...? Is he there? Was I right?

(WOMAN covers mouthpiece with hand, turns to MAN excitedly.)

WOMAN: They're getting him. They said he's on his way...

(MAN *smiles.*)

MAN: And you already had him buried.

WOMAN: *(Exuberant)* I can hear his footsteps.

MAN: How nice. *(Then grabs the receiver from her hand and slams it down)*

WOMAN: What are you doing?!

MAN: Just remembered something....

WOMAN: Give that back to me. My husband...they said...

(MAN *viciously disconnects phone and hands it to* LARS.)

MAN: I just remembered that visiting time for spouses was last week. Isn't that right, Lars?

LARS: That's correct, sir.

(LARS *and* MAN *chuckle.* LARS *deposits phone in wastebasket.*)

MAN: Of course you're welcome to try again in.... what...what is it...?

LARS: *(Consulting calendar)* Two weeks, sir.

MAN: ...in two weeks. Yes. But we can't guarantee he'll still be here...your husband. He is you husband, isn't he? You did say he's your husband?

(Another plane passes overhead.)

(Silence. Birds chirping)

(MAN *picks up binoculars, briefly studies the birds.*)

MAN: Till then, if I may be bold enough to suggest, you should try listening to the birds. After the planes have all passed and the sky's gone all quiet and clear, you can almost hear them beating their wings. It's a lovely sound when you get to hear it. Always makes me think of where exactly they're off to. Those birds. Really very relaxing. Care to have a look...?

(MAN *offers* WOMAN *the binoculars. She doesn't take them.*)

(*Lights fade.*)

END OF PLAY